CHINA FOCUS
CHINESE CULTURE

Edited by Charlotte Guillain

Heinemann Library
Chicago, Illinois

Customer Service   888–454–2279

Visit our website at www.heinemannlibrary.com

Designed by Richard Parker and Manhattan Design
Printed by China Translation Printing Services

12 11 10 09 08
10 9 8 7 6 5 4 3 2 1

Library of Congress Cataloging-in-Publication Data
Guillain, Charlotte.
   Chinese culture / Charlotte Guillain. -- 1st ed.
      p. cm. -- (China focus)
   Includes bibliographical references and index.
   ISBN-13: 978-1-4329-1218-5 (hc)
   1. China--Civilization--Juvenile literature. I. Title.
DS721.G889 2008
306.0951--dc22
                            2007049477

Acknowledgments
The publishers would like to thank the following for permission to reproduce photographs:
©Corbis pp. **9** (Carl & Ann Purcell), **11** (Wolfgang Koehler), **12** (Keren Su), **13** (Tiziana and Gianni Baldizzone), **15** (Asian Art & Archaeology, Inc.), **16** (Christie's Images), **17** (Massimo Mastrorillo), **19** (David G. Houser), **21** (Bojan Brecelj), **22** (Keren Su), **23** (AFP/Earl & Nazima Kowall), **28** (Vince Streano), **29** (Michael S. Yamashita), **31** (George Shelley), **33** (Wolfgang Koehler), **36** (Studio Eye), **37** (Bohemian Nomad Picturemakers), **38** (epa/Michael Reynolds), **39** (Ryan Pyle); ©Getty Images pp. **8** (AFP/Mike Clarke), **25** (Evan Agostini), **34** (National Geographic); ©The Kobal Collection (Beijing New Picture/Elite Group) p. **26**; ©Pearson Education Ltd (David Rigg) p **7**; ©Photolibrary pp. **6** (Imagestate Ltd), **10** (Pacific Stock), **20** (Hemis), **32** (Botanica), **40** (Australian Only); ©WTPix p. **41**.

Cover photograph of the Beijing Opera reproduced with permission of ©Alamy (Viewstock).

The publishers would like to thank Clare Hibbert, Ali Brownlie Bojang, Melanie Guile, Jane Shuter, Dale Anderson, Neil Morris, and Jameson Anderson for additional material.

Contents

Some words are printed in bold, **like this**. You can find out what they mean by looking in the glossary.

Introduction to China

China is a huge country that stretches from Europe in the west to the Pacific Ocean in the east. The Chinese are very proud of their ancient nation, which has a **culture** that has developed over thousands of years.

What is culture?

Culture is a people's way of living. It is the way a group of people makes itself separate and different from any other group. Culture includes a group's spoken and written language, social **customs**, and habits, as well as its traditions of art, craft, dance, drama, music, literature, and religion. This book explores different aspects of Chinese art and culture, looking at examples from different moments in China's history and from different regions.

The people

China's population is over 1.3 billion people, which is one-fifth the world's population. Most of the people in China are Han Chinese. Han people share the same written language but speak different **dialects**, such as **Cantonese**. **Mandarin** is the most common spoken Chinese. A large number of **ethnic minorities** live in China, including the Zhuang, Manchu, Hui, Miao, and Uyghur.

Government

China is ruled by one political party. This is the Chinese **Communist** Party. Mao Zedong was the first Communist leader who led China through "the **Cultural Revolution**" (1966-1976). This wiped out centuries of cultural tradition in China. **Monasteries**, temples, and galleries were burned; artists, writers, musicians, and performers were killed or banished. Since the end of the Cultural Revolution, traditional arts have been brought back to life and now the government is starting to support Chinese culture and arts.

RUSSIA

MONGOLIA

KAZAKHSTAN

KYRGYZSTAN

GOBI DESERT

Harbin

NORTH
KOREA

JAPAN

*TAKLIMAKAN
DESERT*

CHINA

Beijing
Tianjin

SOUTH
KOREA

*YELLOW
SEA*

PAKISTAN

*TIBETAN
PLATEAU*

HIMALAYAS

NEPAL

Mt Everest

BHUTAN

BANGLADESH

INDIA

MYANMAR
(BURMA)

Xi'an

Chengdu

Huang He River

Chang Jiang River

Chongqing

GUIZHOU

YUNNAN

Shenzhen

VIETNAM

LAOS

Shanghai

EAST
CHINA
SEA

TAIWAN

Guangzhou

HONG
KONG

HAINAN

*SOUTH
CHINA
SEA*

PHILIPPINES

N
W · E
S

0 ———— 600 miles
0 ———— 1000 km

All the colored areas on this map show
the provinces of modern China.

Traditions

Many ancient **traditions** still are strong in daily life in China. These traditions include respecting elders and **ancestors**, avoiding shame or humiliation, sharing food after hard work, and finding peace in nature and joy in festivals.

CHINESE CALENDAR

The Chinese calendar runs on a 12-year cycle known as the Chinese zodiac. Each year is allotted a different animal. The year of the dragon is especially lucky. Here is the zodiac for the current cycle:

2008—rat
2009—ox
2010—tiger
2011—rabbit
2012—dragon
2013—snake
2014—horse
2015—goat
2016—monkey
2017—rooster
2018—dog
2019—pig

Chinese New Year

Southern China's main holiday is Spring Festival (*Chun Jie*) or Chinese New Year. It is held in late January or early February and everyone celebrates the new beginning. People clean their houses, buy new clothes, pay back any money they owe, and settle arguments. People think about their ancestors and have family gatherings. A highlight of this festival is the dragon dance in the streets, when noisy firecrackers are let off to scare evil spirits away. This is for good luck in the coming year. Many people use the holiday to travel and visit relatives and all tourist spots are busy at New Year.

The dragon dance is a famous image of China that is known throughout the world.

Moon Festival

Moon Festival (*Zhong qiu Jie*) is a harvest celebration, held in September or early October. Special moon cakes are cooked and eaten together with pomelo fruit, a large pear-shaped citrus fruit that ripens in autumn. Fireworks are let off and people give moon cakes as presents. Moon cakes traditionally have a filling made of seed paste.

RECIPE FOR MOON CAKES

You will need:
- pastry
- rolling pin
- jam
- round cookie cutter
- flat baking tray
- spatula

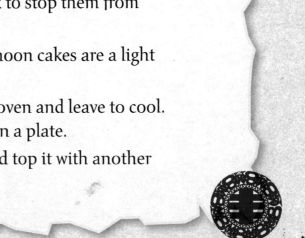

1. Roll out the pastry so it is $\frac{1}{2}$ inch (0.5 cm) thick. Use the cookie cutter to cut out circles of dough.

2. Place the circles of dough on a baking tray.

3. Prick the dough circles with a fork to stop them from puffing while cooking.

4. Bake at 350°F (180°C) until the moon cakes are a light golden brown color.

5. Remove the baking tray from the oven and leave to cool. When cool, put the moon cakes on a plate.

6. Spread jam on one moon cake and top it with another moon cake.

Dragon Boat Festival

The Dragon Boat Festival (*Duanwu Jie*) is held in mid-summer. This festival celebrates the memory of Qu Yuan, a poet who drowned himself around 300 BCE. Everybody eats rice dumplings steamed in leaves. People race boats that are painted to look like dragons. While they race, they beat drums to frighten away evil spirits.

This photograph shows boat racing at the Dragon Boat Festival.

Lantern Festival

At the Lantern Festival (*Yuanxiao Jie*), held early in the year, people make or buy beautiful paper lanterns. When evening comes, they light them and gather in the streets and parks.

Ox Soul Festival

The Zhuang people use oxen to help them work in the fields. But all oxen rest during the Ox Soul Festival, when the Zhuang celebrate the birthday of the Ox King. The oxen are fed steamed black rice to make sure the Ox King brings a good harvest.

Traditional clothes

Clothes in China also follow many traditions. The Chinese have been making fine clothes since around 2600 BCE, when silk first was made using the thread of the silkworm. Ethnic groups in southwest China also are famous for their hand-crafted clothes. People in the countryside still make many traditional fabrics, including prints, embroidery, **pleating**, lace, and braids.

Changing fashions

In southern China women traditionally wear the *qipao*. This is a fitted, silk women's dress with a high collar and slit skirt. It was worn traditionally with pants. After 1949, the Communist government banned traditional dress and replaced it with the loose-fitting "Mao suit" and cap for both women and men.

Today, Western fashion is popular. In the cities, people wear jeans and business suits. International fashion shows are held every year in the cities of Shanghai and Beijing. In the country, however, **peasants** in the warmer south still wear traditional cone-shaped hats, plain loose jackets, and pants.

This factory worker is bundling up rolls of silk thread.

COLORFUL TRADITIONS

The colors people wear have important meanings in China. Red stands for happiness and good luck. Chinese brides often get married in red. Blue is the color of power and favored by men.

Ethnic Groups

China has many different ethnic groups, mostly close to the country's borders. About 100 million people belong to these minority groups. They see themselves as being very different from the Han Chinese. It can be difficult for the government to make all Chinese people feel part of the same country. For example, many areas, such as Tibet, want to keep their own culture and traditions. Many minority people generally do not accept Chinese rule.

The Kazakhs

The Kazakhs were horsemen who rode around the large plains of central Asia with their herds. Today, over a million Kazakhs live in the province of Xinjiang. Some are farmers, but many still live in felt tents, called yurts. They speak their own language and do not write with Chinese **script**. They follow the Muslim **religion**.

These women are wearing traditional Tibetan dress.

The Uyghurs

The Uyghurs of Xinjiang see themselves as Turkish, not Asian. They eat lamb kebab and wheat flatbread, foods that are different from those eaten in other parts of China. They also have their own folktales, as well as a special type of opera called *The 12 Mukams*. This opera includes 340 classical songs and folk dances, **accompanied** by strings and tambourines. They have their own way of writing and they are Muslim.

The Jinuo

Around 18,000 Jinuo people live in the mountains of Yunnan. They have no written language, only a spoken language. Traditionally, up to 20 families shared large, thatched-roofed huts built on stilts.

The Jinuo worship nature and the sun, and perform their Big Drum Dance (*Echeguo*) for the harvest spirits. They are known for their stretched earlobes plugged with thick bamboo sticks or flowers. Women wear white hoods and striped tunics in seven bold colors.

This Jinuo girl is wearing traditional costume.

BLACK TEETH

Traditionally, Jinuo people make their teeth black with pear-tree **sap**. They believe this is very beautiful.

The Miao

The Miao are famous for their weaving, **batik**, and embroidery skills. Miao wear fabrics in striking reds, blues, and whites on black cloth. Their full pleated skirts, embroidered aprons, and decorated hats are a brilliant sight. An ancient Miao folktale explains their bright clothing. A young hunter brought a pheasant home to his mother. She loved the color and beauty of the bird, so she made a costume to match it. The bird's head crest became the tall headpiece, its wings were the richly embroidered sleeves, its tail became the short pleated skirt and belt, and its legs were the colored leg-wrappings.

These Miao people from Guizhou Province are in traditional costume. The women's headdresses are made of woven human hair. The ribbons and cloth are all hand-woven by the women and girls.

WEDDING PANTS

The Yi people of Yunnan make a special wedding costume. The bride sews a pair of pants for her groom, but she stitches up the leg openings. At the celebration, the groom has to force his feet into the pants as quickly as he can. He then wears them every day until the first child is born. The pants then are used as a wrap for the baby.

The Dong

The Dong of southern China wear embroidered sashes, caps, ribbons, and braids. Dong babies wear brightly decorated caps to ward off evil spirits. The spirits are supposed to think the caps are flowers and pass them by.

The Dong people still live in traditional two-story houses. Animals and firewood are kept on the lower floor, while the family lives on the upper floor.

Each Dong village has a spectacular tower, up to 13 stories high. The tower looks like a fir tree from a distance, because of its many overlapping roofs. Fir trees are **sacred** to the Dong people. The villagers paint the tower to show **myths**, legends, and scenes of everyday life.

This photo shows a drum tower in a Dong village.

18—YEAR TREES

To celebrate the birth of a new child, Dong parents plant a group of pine trees. They call these "18-year trees," because the trees will be ready to cut down 18 years later, when the child becomes an adult. The trees will supply enough pine timber to build a home for this adult.

Visual Arts

Pottery and ceramics

The Chinese started to use a wheel to make pottery from clay around 4,000 years ago. Around 600 CE, they discovered how to make porcelain from a fine white clay. Elsewhere in the world, **porcelain** is often called "china," because this is where it first came from.

Stone Age pottery

Even before they invented the potter's wheel, the Chinese were skilled potters. They coiled "snakes" of clay into dishes or shaped the clay by hand. People who lived at Banpo between 5000 and 4000 BCE are known as the "painted pottery" people, because of their decorated **earthenware** pots.

Tomb pottery

During Qin and Han times, important people often were buried with pottery copies of their belongings. They thought that they might need these things in the next life. Many tombs contain clay models of buildings, as well as rice fields, fishponds, and wells. Some tombs also have miniature farm animals, farm workers, servants, soldiers, and entertainers.

Statues

Chinese potters have made beautiful **ceramic** statues. Many old **Buddhist** temples include large painted figures. These huge statues were **fired** as single pieces in enormous kilns (ovens).

CHINESE CLAYS

Different types of clay are found in China:

- Loess is a brownish-yellow clay from northern China, used for **terracotta** figures and pots.
- The finest type of clay is white china clay, called kaolin, which comes from southern China.

This Ming Dynasty porcelain jar dates back to the 1500s and is decorated with bright colors. Less-expensive jars were used for storage, but this jar was probably an ornament. Ming porcelain is very valuable today.

Decorating porcelain

Porcelain first was developed during the Tang **Dynasty** (618–906 CE). It was white, thin, and almost see-through. By the time of the Yuan Dynasty (1279–1368 CE), the first blue and white porcelain was being produced.

During Ming times (1368–1644 CE), workers in the city of Jingdezhen produced pure white porcelain decorated with hand-painted birds and flowers in blue. In the 1500s, artists painted scenes of human figures in green, red, and blue. Today, Jingdezhen has dozens of high-tech porcelain factories, a porcelain research institute, and a museum of porcelain.

Painting

Traditional Chinese art often shows peace and **harmony** between people and nature. This idea was part of the Daoist religion (see page 28). Many Chinese artists painted simple lines on plain backgrounds, using color only lightly. Painters used ink and brushes on fine paper (called *xuan*) or silk. Paintings often show landscapes, portraits, and detailed studies of nature.

Old Masters

The first great Chinese artist was Gu Kaizhi, who lived around 344–406 CE. He is most famous for his **calligraphy**.

Wang Wei (699–759 CE) was a famous poet and musician as well as a painter. He became an artist at the emperor's **court**. Many people like his black ink landscapes because of their magical atmosphere of mist and water.

Pan Tianshou (1897–1971) created beautiful paintings of birds, insects, and flowers, which are in galleries around the world.

Artist Zhou Xianji painted these plum blossoms and sparrows in ink on paper in the 1600s.

Calligraphy is a highly respected Chinese tradition.

Calligraphy

In China, the skill of writing is an art form, called calligraphy. In Chinese writing, each **character** is a kind of word picture and in China the arts of painting and calligraphy are closely linked. In both, the brush strokes and use of ink are important.

Calligraphy has "four treasures": paper; the ink stick (which makes ink when water is added); the ink stone (for mixing the ink); and brushes. The same tools are used for traditional Chinese painting. Calligraphy uses many different styles or scripts, but the flow, grace, and **flair** of the brush strokes are always important. People still see calligraphy as a very special skill and use it today on banners, flags, paintings, and in temples.

PAPER

Around 100 CE, the Chinese invented paper. The first paper was very expensive. The paper was made of silk fibers squeezed together. Soon, paper was made by mashing plants and rags with water and pressing them together. This made paper cheaper and stronger.

Performing Arts

Music

The government in China strongly supports traditional Chinese music, which is taught and performed in academies all over the country. Western classical music is also popular in the cities and many of the world's great classical performers have come from China. Pop music is very popular, particularly in the city of Hong Kong, which was a British colony until 1997. Interest in rock and punk is growing as well.

Traditional

Chinese music uses a five-tone **scale**, not an eight-tone scale as in Western music. The sounds of traditional Chinese music are complicated and subtle. A traditional orchestra is divided into four groups: strings played with a bow; plucked strings; flutes; and percussion (mostly **gongs** and kettle drums). Among the plucked strings are the zithers, including the ancient seven-stringed *guqin*, which noblemen once had to learn. A traditional orchestra accompanies Chinese opera.

Pop and rock

In Chinese pop music, solo female artists and male bands are very popular. Andy Lau is a Hong Kong-based singer and actor who has become a superstar all over China. Faye Wong has a quirky, elf-like style and is very popular. She was married to another pop star, Dou Wei, who became famous for "tricking" fans by lip-synching (moving his lips to recorded music) at concerts instead of singing live.

Cui Jian brought hard rock to China at a 1986 concert with his song "Nothing to my Name." The song became an **anthem** for students in the 1980s. Cui always wears a white baseball cap and he often has been banned by the government because of his political beliefs.

Tang Dynasty was the first Chinese heavy metal band. The band's first CD is a mixture of traditional Chinese **opera** and heavy metal. Other styles of music, such as punk rock, disco, and hip hop, are popular and are played in Beijing's nightclubs.

In this photograph, a young Naxi man plays the *pipa*. The Naxi people are descended from **Tibetan nomads**.

Opera

Long ago, traveling groups of actors performed operas and their performances could go on for days. Today, the best-known style of opera in China is Beijing opera. Other styles have developed in different parts of the country, each with its own traditions, costume styles, and stories.

Each opera tells a well-known story. The actors' **elaborate** costumes and colorful makeup tell the audience what kinds of characters they are playing. Usual characters include gods, warriors, clowns, and lovers.

A Chinese opera is accompanied by music from a range of instruments, including drums, bamboo flutes, the *sheng* (mouth organ), and the *pipa* (lute). Dramatic moments often are marked by loud cymbal clashes.

This opera singer's painted face tells us about his character.

MAKEUP

All the actors in a Chinese opera wear colorful and dramatic makeup. For actors playing the parts of gods or warriors, makeup is especially important. The color of the character's face tells the audience about the character's personality. A red face means loyalty, black means the character is serious, white can mean cruel, and yellow means the character is likely to act without thinking.

These rod puppets are backstage at a puppet theater in Shanghai.

Puppetry

China has three different types of puppetry. Rod puppets are worked from below using thin metal rods. Shadow puppets are made of finely cut leather, and the audience sees the puppets' shadows appear behind a lit screen. String puppets (marionettes) are worked from above by the puppeteer, who appears on stage. Marionettes are carved in wood and have up to 30 strings. Quanzhou Puppet Troupe, run for 50 years by the great puppet master Huang Yi Que, is the most famous marionette theater in China.

Drama

Western-style drama existed during the 1920s and 1930s in China, but World War II stopped its development. In 1952, the Beijing People's Art Theater was set up by actor and playwright Cao Yu (1910–1996). He wrote classic plays, such as *Sunrise*, *Wasteland*, and *Beijingers*, which still are performed today. Lao She (1899–1966) is the country's best-loved playwright. His work *Teahouse* is perhaps China's most famous play. He died during the Cultural Revolution (1966–1976).

Hong Kong is a busy center of modern drama. Tang Shu-wing is famous around the world as a theater director and actor. His theater company "No Man's Land" produces works that include puppets, video, and other multimedia techniques.

Dance

Dance is an important part of Chinese culture. Dancing is used to entertain people and to mark special occasions. It is also one of the key ingredients of Chinese opera.

New Year celebrations

Chinese dancers mark celebrations throughout the year, but the most famous dances are performed at New Year. Two of the most popular New Year dances are the lion dance and the dragon dance.

The lion dance

Two dancers take part in the lion dance, one at the head of the costume and one at the tail. The lion traditionally is made of silk, with silken tassels. Sometimes its face can be controlled from inside the head, so the dancer can make the lion open and close its eyes.

The dancers are accompanied by percussion instruments such as drums, cymbals, and gongs. Near the end of the dance, the lion pretends to eat the lucky bundle of leaves and money that is hanging from a doorway, then spits out the leaves. This is a sign that there will be plenty of food and riches in the year ahead.

A pair of lions performs the lion dance at these New Year celebrations in Beijing, China's capital.

Acrobatics were being performed in China around 500 BCE and are still very popular. Chinese acrobats are spectacular athletes and are trained from earliest childhood.

The dragon dance

The other dance that brings good luck for the coming year is the dragon dance. Some dragons are extremely long, with 50 people or more controlling them. The dancers leap and crouch to the beat of the drum. Skillful dancers can make the dragon form special patterns. These have names such as "cloud cave" or "going around the pillar."

Other dances

China has many other traditional dances as well. Waist-drum dancing is popular in parts of northern China. The dancers usually dress as soldiers and make the beat of their drums sound like horses' hooves.

The fan dance used to be performed by dancing girls to entertain the emperor. Each dancer would hold a fan and make special arm movements, while the rest of her body hardly moved. Dances like these still are performed sometimes on national holidays.

DRAGONS

In China, the dragon is an important symbol of supernatural power. During celebrations, people often wave a paper dragon with a pearl in its mouth. The pearl represents wisdom and light.

Books, Film, and Television

Writing

Writing is so important in China that the Chinese word for culture is *wenhua*, which means "to be able to read and write." Chinese written records stretch back 3,000 years, longer than those of any other culture in the world.

There has been a record of poems and stories being written in China since around 1000 BCE, when song **lyrics** by an unknown author were collected in a book called the *Shijing*. Another collection, the *Songs of Chu*, was composed around 200 BCE. These works became the great classics of Chinese poetry.

Novels appeared in China in about 1400 CE. They became very popular. *Journey to the West* (or *Monkey*) by Wu Cheng'en is a book based on the life of a Buddhist **monk** called Xuan Zang, who travels to India. Animal and spirit companions travel with him and their adventures make a lively story. *Dream of Red Mansions*, written around 1760 by Cao Xueqin, is a very famous novel about a large, wealthy family in Beijing.

Literature today

Until about 1900, most literature in China was written in an ancient language called *wenyan* or *guwen*, which only **scholars** could understand. In the early 1900s, however, writers began to produce works in everyday script. Lu Xun (1881–1936) is famous as the father of modern Chinese literature. He wrote bleak short stories such as *Diary of a Madman* and *The Story of Ah Q*. Lao She (1899–1966) wrote about the desperate poverty of Beijing street life in *Rickshaw Boy*.

Punk Lit

Wang Shuo (born 1958) is the best-known of a group of new young writers called the Punk Lit Group. He has written more than 20 novels, as well as film and television scripts. His topics are often violent and tough, with criminals and homeless people as main characters.

In 2000, the writer Gao Xingjian won the Nobel Prize for Literature, an international award. Some of his novels have been banned in China for criticizing the government. He left China in 1987 and now lives in France.

Film

Chinese films were made during the 1930s and 1940s, mostly in Shanghai. Often these films told the story of war in China. During the Cultural Revolution (1966–1976), the Communist government banned all filmmaking that did not agree with its ideas.

Chen Huaikai was a famous filmmaker working when Mao Zedong was leader. During the Cultural Revolution, he was criticized and handed over to the government by his own 14-year-old son. The government banned him from working for 10 years. His son, Chen Kaige, was sorry for what he had done, and is today one of China's most famous and successful filmmakers. He won first prize at the Cannes Film Festival in France for his film *Farewell My Concubine* in 1993.

His friend, the director Zhang Yimou (born 1950), is admired around the world for his sensitive, brilliantly shot films, including *Raise the Red Lantern* (1991).

In recent years, Chinese cinema has become more popular in the West. Zhang Yimou's 2002 film *Hero* was an international success.

KUNG-FU MOVIES

Hong Kong "kung-fu" films are popular throughout Asia. These adventure movies featuring superheroes with magical powers are called *Wu Xia* films in Hong Kong. Jackie Chan is the best-known maker of and performer in these films.

Ang Lee is a director from Taiwan, an island off the southeastern coast of mainland China. His film *Crouching Tiger, Hidden Dragon* was a worldwide hit, winning the Academy Award for Best Foreign Language Film and three other Academy Awards in 2001. *Crouching Tiger, Hidden Dragon* made several Chinese-speaking actors famous in the West, including Chow Yun-Fat, Michelle Yeoh, Zhang Ziyi, and Chang Chen. The story is of a warrior's search for his stolen magical sword.

Television

Most houses in China have a television. Most programs are made by the government-run Chinese Central Television (CCTV) and content is strictly controlled. Programs include news, drama, crime shows, documentaries, and light entertainment, but the most popular are the locally made soap operas. Chinese TV does include advertisements and foreign shows, but these often are **censored**.

TELEVISION IN CHINA

More than 96 percent of the population in China has access to television, which has more than 50 channels.

Religion, Beliefs, and Customs

Under Communist law, China has no religion, but **Daoism**, **Confucianism**, Buddhism, Christianity, and Islam are followed widely. Daoism was founded by Laozi around 600 BCE and is based on the idea of Dao (the Way), meaning life and nature in harmony. Confucius was a **philosopher** whose moral and social laws became the Confucian religion.

Buddhism

Siddhartha Gautama (c. 485–405 BCE) was an Indian prince who later became known as the Buddha, or the Enlightened One. He founded the religion of Buddhism, which reached China around 60 CE.

Buddhists believe that they can achieve a state of supreme happiness, called nirvana, through **meditation** and by following the Eightfold Path. This is a set of eight rules that help people to live better lives. The Chinese developed their own four branches of Buddhism. Buddhism was most popular in China during the Tang dynasty (600s to 900s CE).

China has more than 13,000 Buddhist temples. This one is in Yunnan Province.

This man is visiting his ancestor's grave. He is lighting sweet-smelling sticks (incense) at the graveside.

Ancestor worship

Most Chinese people have great respect for their ancestors. These are their dead relatives. The ancient Chinese believed that the spirits of the dead went to an **afterlife** that was just like ordinary life. People believed that these spirits could decide what happened to their relatives still living on Earth. Therefore, the ancient Chinese looked after family tombs carefully, leaving offerings for dead family members. They also prayed to them. Today, many people still leave gifts at their ancestors' graves. They hope their ancestors will help them in some way. Ancestors especially are **honored** at Chinese New Year to bring peace and good fortune to the family.

Yin and yang

Many Chinese people believe that everything in the universe can be explained as a balance between *yang* and *yin*. Yang represents energy and light and is a male force. *Yin*, the opposite of *yang*, is still, dark, and female.

Many aspects of Chinese culture try to keep this balance. Every morning, people exercise with the slow movements of *tai chi* to prepare their bodies and spirits for the busy day. People cook food with the correct balance of "heating" and "cooling" foods to stay healthy. Chinese people generally try to find harmony within themselves and with others in all sides of their lives.

Feng shui

Feng shui is a way of living based on ancient Chinese **philosophies**. It has become popular in the West in recent years. Followers of *feng shui*, which means "wind and water," try to order their lives and possessions in order to achieve perfect harmony. *Feng shui* experts help design buildings to make sure there is a flow of positive energies.

Chinese medicine

Traditional Chinese medicine (*zhongyi*) is based on the flow of energy, or *qi* ("chee"), around the body. If you are well, your energy flows smoothly. If you are unwell, the energy is blocked in some way. Traditional Chinese doctors believe that what you eat, how you exercise, and how you think affect your *qi*. The aim of all Chinese medicine is to get your *qi* flowing well.

Many people in China today prefer traditional methods of treating illnesses to modern drugs or surgery. Doctors use many herbs to cure illnesses and sometimes these herbal medicines have fewer **side effects** than modern drugs. Chinese medicine concentrates on the welfare of the whole person, with herbal remedies and **acupuncture** as well as Western-style drugs.

Acupuncture is a popular traditional Chinese remedy. A doctor inserts needles into various points on the patient's body. Each point is linked to a different part of the body. For example, blood circulation problems can be treated by applying needles to the feet. Acupuncture should only be performed by a qualified doctor.

Acupuncture is inserting needles into the body at exact "points" to get the *qi* flowing again.

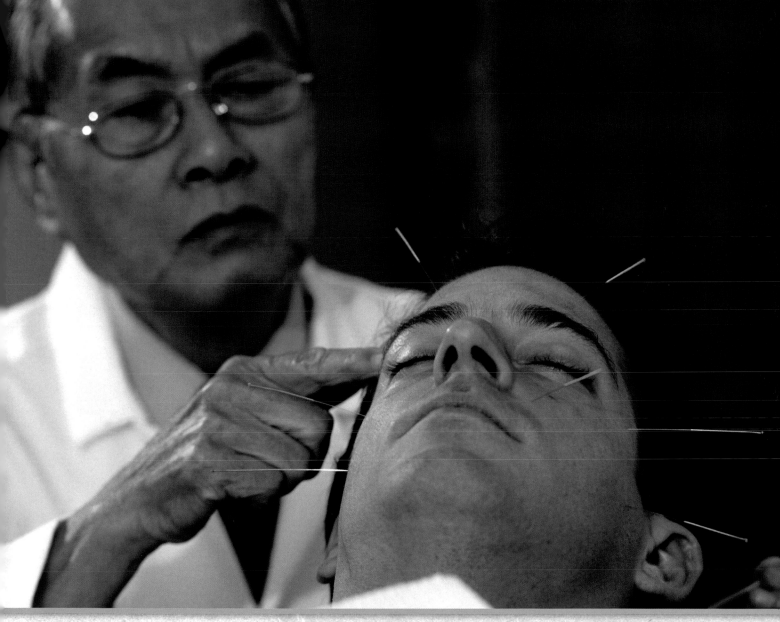

HERBAL CURES

Ancient Chinese herbal cures still are in use in the 21st century. For example, the ancient Chinese ate willow bark for pain relief. Modern aspirin is a chemical version of willow bark.

Family and Daily Life

Traditionally, the family in China always has been very special. In ancient China, the most important member of a family was the oldest man. Even today, fathers still lead the family unit and make most decisions.

Women

The Confucian religion taught that women and girls should be obedient to husbands and fathers. Throughout Chinese history, women have generally been second to men. Wife-selling and **arranged marriages** were common. From around 1000 CE until 1911, rich women's feet were broken and tightly wrapped with "foot-binding" bandages to make them smaller. Tiny feet were supposed to be more beautiful.

The Communists banned foot binding, made primary education a requirement for girls and boys, and offered basic health care to all. Women started to do paid work, and many have senior jobs. Under the Communists, women's lives have gotten better, although men still have the most power.

The family still comes first in China today.

This poster in Shanghai is advertising China's One Child Policy.

Women and girls today still are not equal to men and boys. Women are paid less than men and they mostly work low-paying, uninteresting jobs. Many country girls are kept home to help on the farms, when they should be at school.

Children

The Chinese leader Deng Xiaoping launched the One Child Policy in 1979. This made it illegal for couples to have more than one child. China's population was growing quickly and the government wanted to slow it down. The government gives families with one child extra money, better health care, and better education. People who have more children can be punished with large fines. In recent years, the government has become less strict and most peasants are allowed two children, especially if the first child is a girl. Many parents want a boy to help bring in money for the family.

BABY BOYS

Many boys in China are spoiled. They can become overweight through eating too much. There are many more boys in China than girls. This is a problem because there are not enough women for young men to marry.

Education

Throughout history, the Chinese have respected and valued scholars. For thousands of years, however, most Chinese people had no access to education. School was only for the rich. However, when the Communist government took control of China in 1949, its leader Mao Zedong wanted all people to be treated equally. Every child now had to go to primary school.

Today in China, all young people between ages six and 16 are supposed to go to school. Class sizes often are large and children have to take exams at the end of primary and secondary school. Over 90 percent of the population can read and write. Children study hard, because people believe that they will shame their families if they fail exams.

The school day in China runs from 7:45 a.m. until 4:00 p.m., five days a week.

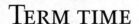

TERM TIME

China has two school terms: September to January and March to July.

Work

About 45 percent of people in China live in the countryside and work very hard as farmers. Farming is very important in China. It provides food for the country's huge population. People and animals do most of the farm work, but farmers are starting to use machines, such as tractors. This means they can produce more food. Most farming families hope for a son to help on the farm. When daughters get married, they usually go to work on their husband's family's farm.

Migration

Many rural people in China are leaving the countryside to find jobs in the cities. Many poor young women **migrate** from the country to cities, like Beijing and Shanghai, looking for work. City factories are full of women working 12- to 16-hour days and earning low wages in terrible conditions. The factories often give the workers a place to live, but these areas can be overcrowded and dirty. Workers often put up with such bad conditions because they earn much more in the city than they could in the countryside. Many young people send most of their money home to their families.

TIME OFF

China has nine public holidays each year when workers take time off. These holidays are:

January 1:	New Year
January/February:	Chinese New Year
March 8:	International Women's Day
May 1-3:	Labor Day
May 4:	National Youth Day
May 23:	Tibet Liberation Day
June 1:	International Children's Day
August 1:	Army Day
October 1-3:	National Day

Food

Confucius said, "Eating is the first happiness." Eating together is an important part of family life in China. Rice is the basic food in most parts of China. In the north, baked breads, dumplings, and wheat noodles are eaten. The four main styles of food in China, based on the regions they come from, are: Cantonese; Eastern; northern regions; and Sichuan.

Cantonese food

Cantonese food is known throughout the world. The southern coast of Guangdong supplies seafood, fresh vegetables, and an amazing variety of meats, such as chicken, snake, monkey, and dog. Food usually is chopped and steamed, or stir-fried very quickly in lightly flavored sauces. Rice is served with every meal.

This is dim sum, a Cantonese speciality. Dim sum means "to touch the heart."

The Cantonese invented the *dim sum* meal. Tiny pieces of delicious food are cooked in bamboo baskets and wheeled around the restaurant on carts. Diners select dozens of different dishes to try. Chicken feet, pork dumplings, fried sesame parcels, and shark's fin soup are very popular.

Eastern style food

Shanghai and Suzhou styles of cooking have been enjoyed by food-lovers for centuries. Ingredients include clams, carp fish, pork, and chicken, which are stir-fried in delicately flavored sauces. Fresh vegetables and rice contrast with some of the oily meats, such as eel and duck.

Food from northern regions

Rice does not grow so well in the north, so wheat and a grain called millet are used to make dumplings and noodles. Roasted meat, especially lamb, and hot stews are traditional.

Northern dishes tend to be more **starchy** and fatty than other Chinese styles of cooking, to provide energy in the icy winter climate. Steamed pigeon with yam, stir-fried jellyfish, and the well-known Peking duck (crisp-skinned roast duck) are examples of northern-style dishes.

Sichuan style food

Sichuan food, from the region around Chengdu, has become famous around the world for its hot and spicy flavors. Red chilies and other fiery spices like garlic, pepper, and ginger are stir-fried with pork and chicken, which often are **marinated** (soaked) or pickled before cooking.

The Chinese invented tea and drink it with every meal.

Sports

China is a sport-loving country. For example, men's and women's soccer has become very popular in China. The women's World Cup was held in China in 2007. Other popular sports include badminton, gymnastics, and table tennis.

Kung fu

Kung fu is a type of Chinese **martial art**. In China, there are hundreds of different forms of kung fu. The term is not easy to translate, but perhaps the closest meaning is "skill expert." The Chinese word for "martial art" is *wushu*.

All the world's martial arts can be traced back to ancient China, which had a strong influence on Korea, Japan, and the rest of the **Far East**. Chinese clans, families, and individuals learned to defend themselves during many troubled periods in ancient times. All Chinese martial arts are linked to religious or philosophical beliefs.

Tai Chi is a form of exercise that involves slow movement and concentration. It exercises the body and mind.

China underwent a huge development program to get ready for the 2008 Olympic Games.

The Olympics

China won the bid to hold the 2008 Olympic Games in Beijing. The city beat Paris, Istanbul, Osaka, and Toronto to win the Games. The Chinese government was pleased to have this chance to show the rest of the world how well it could run the Olympics. An Olympic Cultural Festival was held in the five years before the Games. Beijing improved its transportation system for the Games, making its airport bigger and developing a high-speed railway.

OLYMPIC SPORTS

At the 2004 Olympic Games in Athens, Chinese athletes won an incredible 32 gold medals in many sports, including:

- athletics
- badminton
- canoeing
- diving
- gymnastics
- judo
- shooting
- swimming
- table tennis
- tae kwon do
- volleyball
- weightlifting
- wrestling

A Global Culture

Culture, the arts, and sports all are flourishing in China today. The government provides money for the Beijing opera, classical Chinese music, puppetry, and folk dance. The Chinese are world champions in many sports and the Olympic Games have led to the development of sports in the country. People across the country enjoy locally made television series, films, and pop music. All of this is linked to the growth of China's economy. Many people have more money than a few years ago and there are fewer people living in poverty today.

However, China is still a poor, crowded, hard-working country and life can be tough for many of the ethnic minorities living there. People in the countryside are still desperately poor and workers in the cities often are **exploited** and made to work in dangerous conditions. The **media** is still strictly censored and any opposition is punished.

Worldwide culture

Chinese culture has spread all over the world. Many cities in different countries have their own Chinatowns, which are areas with Chinese shops and restaurants. Sometimes there are Chinese cinemas and people celebrate Chinese festivals in the streets. Chinese cinema and literature are becoming more and more popular in the West and Chinese athletes are becoming famous on the world stage. Chinese culture goes back thousands of years and seems just as strong today as it ever has been.

Chinatowns, such as this one in Sydney, Australia, are a common sight in cities around the world.

Today, shopping has become a popular pastime in China's big cities. This is a crowded street in Shanghai.

Timeline

5000-4000 BCE
"Painted pottery" people at Banpo make decorated earthenware pots.

c. 2600 BCE
Chinese learn to make silk.

c. 2000 BCE
Chinese learn to make bronze.

1000 BCE
Song lyrics collected into a book called the *Shijing*.

551–479 BCE
The dates when historians think Confucius lived.

500s BCE
The period when historians think Laozi lived.

400s BCE
Metal coins come into use in China.

300s BCE
The *Laozi*, one of the basic books of Daoism, is written down. Gu Kaizhi paints human figures and landscapes.

c. 200 BCE
The *Songs of Chu* are composed.

60 CE
Buddhism reaches China.

105
Traditional date the Chinese give for the invention of paper.

c. 538
Trade with the West via the Silk Road allows Westerners to appreciate Chinese art.

c. 600
Porcelain is invented and perfected in China.

960–1279
The Song Dynasty rules China.

c.1000
Paper is first used as a painting surface.

1271
Blue and white porcelain becomes very popular.

1368–1644
The Ming Dynasty rules China.

c.1570
Journey to the West is written by Wu Cheng'en.

c.1760
Dream of Red Mansions is written by Cao Xueqin.

1839–1842
China is at war with Britain.

1897
The painter Pan Tianshou is born.

1911
Foot binding is banned.

1949
People's Republic of China is established. Communist government bans traditional dress.

1952
Beijing People's Art Theater is set up by actor and playwright Cao Yu.

1958
The writer Wang Shuo is born.

1966–1976
The Cultural Revolution takes place. During this time, schools are closed and young people are encouraged to rebel against the system.

1976
Mao Zedong dies.

1978
Economic reforms begin.

1979
The One Child Policy is launched.

1989
There are demonstrations for democracy in Tiananmen Square. Cui Jian performs in the square, singing pro-democracy songs.

1993
Farewell My Concubine wins first prize at the Cannes Film Festival.

1997
Britain returns Hong Kong to China.

2000
The writer Gao Xingjian wins the Nobel prize for Literature.

2001
China is awarded the 2008 Summer Olympic Games. *Crouching Tiger, Hidden Dragon* wins Oscar for Best Foreign Language film.

2004
Chinese athletes win 32 gold metals at the Olympic Games in Athens.

2007
China hosts the women's soccer World Cup.

2008
Beijing hosts the 2008 Summer Olympic Games.

Glossary

accompany to play music with

acupuncture medical treatment in which needles are put into the body at certain points to cure illnesses

afterlife where some people believe you go when you die

ancestor someone who lived before you in your family, who is dead now

anthem popular song

arranged marriage wedding organized by the bride and groom's families

batik decorative fabric made by painting melted wax onto fabric

Buddhism religion based on the teachings of the Buddha

calligraphy art and skill of writing

Cantonese dialect spoken in parts of China

censorship act of preventing people from expressing ideas and opinions

ceramic material shaped and then hardened by firing (usually pottery)

characters picture-like symbols used in Chinese writing

Communist belonging to a political system called Communism

Confucianism belief system started by Confucius

court where the emperor lives

Cultural Revolution (1966-1976) campaign by Communist Party Chairman Mao to get rid of his enemies and enforce the strict attitudes and values of the revolution. Thousands of artists, teachers, and writers were killed, tortured, or imprisoned by the government.

culture actions and beliefs of a society

customs usual way of behaving in a certain situation

Daoism religion based on the ideas of Laozi, combined with the ideas of Buddha

dialects variety of a language that is spoken in a particular region

dynasty families who rule an area for more than one generation

earthenware type of pottery

elaborate carefully detailed and exact

ethnic minorities groups of people who share culture and language. These groups are a small percentage of the total population.

exploit use for profit

Far East countries of East Asia

fire bake ceramics in a special oven, called a kiln

flair natural ability or talent

gong bronze musical instrument

harmony state of agreement

honor respect

lyrics words to songs

Mandarin China's official language

marinate soak meat or fish in a sauce before cooking

martial art traditional training of body and mind to keep self-control

media radio, television, newspapers, and the Internet

meditation calming the mind by focusing attention on something simple, such as breathing

migrate move to another area or country, often for work

monastery religious building where monks live

monk male member of a religion living in a special way, apart from other people

myths traditional tales

nomad person who moves from place to place in a group

novel fiction book

opera play set to music that is sung

peasant poor worker in the countryside

philosopher someone who studies the purpose of life

philosophy way of thinking about the world

pleat fold made by doubling cloth on itself

porcelain type of pottery made with kaolin

religion system of belief or worship

sacred holy

sap fluid in a tree or plant

scale series of notes in music

scholar someone who studies a particular subject

script handwriting

side effects problems caused in addition to the intended effect

starchy food rich in carbohydrates

terracotta baked clay

Tibetan from Tibet

tradition passing down of customs, culture, and beliefs

Further Information

Books

Guile, Melanie. *Culture in China*. Chicago: Heinemann Library, 2003.

Salas, Laura Purdie. *China*. Mankato: Capstone Press, 2006.

Sheen, Barbara. *Foods of China*. Chicago: KidHaven Press, 2006.

Places to visit

Many museums have good Chinese collections. Here are some of the more famous ones:

The Metropolitan Museum of Art
1000 5th Ave at 82nd Street
New York, NY 10028-0198
(212) 535-7710 www.metmuseum.org

The Art Institute of Chicago
111 South Michigan Ave
Chicago, IL 60603
(312) 443-3600 www.artic.edu

Asian Art Museum of San Francisco
200 Larkin Street
San Francisco, CA 94102
(415) 581-3500 www.asianart.org

Websites

China Knowledge

www.chinaknowledge.de

This is a website with a wide variety of information on history, art, and culture for people studying China.

Beijing 2008

http://en.beijing2008.cn/

This is the official website of the Beijing 2008 Olympic Games.

Chinese Culture Center of San Francisco

www.c-c-c.org

This organization in San Francisco has information about Chinese and Chinese American art, history, and culture in the United States.

Index